HARVESTING SUCCESS

From Field to Fortune: A Farmer's Guide to Growing Your Business

Olisa Nnadi

Faithdrivenfarmer

Dedication

Dedicated to those who dare to dream, who plant seeds of faith in every endeavor, and who find strength in resilience. May this guide inspire and uplift you on your journey.

Preface

I believe in the power of stories. Stories not only inspire us; they connect us to the experiences of others, revealing the common threads that weave through our journeys. This book is a reflection of my own path, a journey shaped by faith, resilience, and the lessons learned from both my successes and failures in agriculture and business. As a farmer and entrepreneur, I've faced numerous challenges that tested my resolve and commitment. However, it is through these very challenges that I found my voice and purpose. My hope is to share my insights with you, blending practical strategies with spiritual wisdom to empower your own journey. This is not just a guide; it's a conversation, a friendly hand on your shoulder as you navigate the complexities of starting and growing a business.

Whether you are an aspiring entrepreneur or a seasoned business owner, I invite you to join me on this journey of discovery. Together, we will explore the foundations of success, in good stewardship. May this book inspire you to cultivate not just a successful business, but a meaningful life grounded in purpose.

Content

INTRODUCTION

Welcome to a journey that intertwines resilience, and the lessons learned from both successes and setbacks in the world of entrepreneurship. As an entrepreneur rooted in agriculture, particularly in poultry and crop farming, I've come to realize that the principles of business extend far beyond the fields I cultivate. They encompass the essence of who we are, how we navigate challenges, and how we can rise above adversity through unwavering belief in ourselves and our mission.

In this book, I aim to share insights that will not only guide new and seasoned entrepreneurs alike but also inspire you to view your challenges as opportunities for growth. My experiences have taught me that every setback can be transformed into a stepping stone, and each obstacle holds a lesson waiting to be uncovered. Whether you're launching your first venture or looking to revitalize an existing business, my hope is that the stories and strategies within these pages resonate with you.

As you read this book, you will find that the principles of success are universal. They apply across industries, whether you're in technology, retail, or agriculture. Through a faith-driven lens, I will offer practical guidance on understanding market needs, identifying customer desires, and adapting to an ever-changing business landscape. You will see how my reliance on faith has influenced my decision-making during unpredictable times, providing clarity and strength when challenges seemed insurmountable.

Together, let's explore the foundations of successful entrepreneurship, grounded in the belief that with resilience, and a willingness to learn, we can transform our dreams into reality.

LAYING THE FOUNDATION: DEFINING YOUR VISION AND MISSION

Every successful journey begins with a clear destination. As an entrepreneur, defining your vision and mission is akin to laying the cornerstone of your business. It's not just about knowing where you want to go; it's about understanding why you're embarking on this journey in the first place. A well-articulated vision and mission will serve as your guiding star, illuminating your path through the uncertainties of entrepreneurship.

Your vision is your aspirational image of what you want your business to become. It's the big picture, the dream that fuels your passion and motivates you during challenging times. When I started my poultry farm, my vision extended beyond simply producing eggs. I envisioned a sustainable operation that not only provided high-quality products but also contributed positively to my community and the environment. This vision shaped every decision I made, from sourcing feed to engaging with customers. To articulate your vision, ask yourself:

➜ What impact do I want my business to have on my community?

➜ How do I want my business to be perceived in the marketplace? - What legacy do I wish to leave behind?

Writing down your vision statement is a powerful exercise. It solidifies your aspirations and serves as a constant reminder of your purpose. Keep it visible, post it on your wall, include it in your business plan, or even share it with your team. A compelling vision not only inspires you but also resonates with customers, employees, and partners who share your values.

Crafting Your Mission

While your vision paints the picture of your long-term aspirations, your mission defines how you will get there. It articulates the purpose of your business and the core values that will guide your actions. A strong mission statement answers the questions of what you do, whom you serve, and how you do it.

For instance, my mission statement evolved to reflect my commitment to quality, sustainability, and community engagement. It guided my approach to customer service, my choice of suppliers, and my engagement with local initiatives. Each decision I made was a reflection of my mission, ensuring that I remained true to my core values.
When crafting your mission statement, consider:

→ What products or services do I provide, and how do they fulfill customer needs?

→ Who are my target customers, and what value do I bring to them? - What principles or values are non-negotiable for my business?

A mission statement should be concise yet powerful, something you can easily communicate to others. It serves as a rallying cry for your team and a commitment to your customers.

Aligning Values With Actions

Once you've defined your vision and mission, the next step is aligning your daily actions with these foundational elements. This alignment ensures that every decision, from hiring to marketing, reflects your core values and moves you closer to your vision. As I navigated the complexities of running my business, I faced moments of uncertainty that tested my resolve. It was during these times that my faith played a crucial role. I relied on prayer and reflection to guide my decision making, ensuring that my choices aligned with my vision and mission. Faith provided me with clarity and confidence, reminding me that every challenge was an opportunity for growth. Encourage yourself to regularly revisit your vision and mission. Are your current actions still in line with your aspirations? Are there areas where you can improve? By continuously assessing your alignment, you can adapt and evolve your business while staying true to your foundational values.

Building On Solid Ground

Defining your vision and mission is the first step in laying a strong foundation for your entrepreneurial journey. It's a process that requires introspection, honesty, and a commitment to your core values. As you move forward, remember that your vision will guide you through the storms, and your mission will provide clarity amidst the noise. In the chapters ahead, we will explore how to translate this foundation into actionable strategies that lead to success. Embrace the journey ahead, grounded in a clear sense of purpose, and watch as your entrepreneurial dreams take root and flourish.

UNDERSTANDING MARKET NEEDS

Every successful business begins with a deep understanding of market needs. This means recognizing the demands and expectations of consumers and aligning your products or services to meet them. The business landscape is constantly evolving, and the ability to assess and respond to these changes is crucial.

For entrepreneurs, especially those venturing into new markets, the challenge is not just about selling a product; it's about identifying what drives your target audience. Start by conducting thorough market research. This involves not only gathering data but also engaging with your audience. Use surveys, interviews, and focus groups to get firsthand insights into their preferences. What problems are they facing that your business can solve? This knowledge is vital; it allows you to create products or services that genuinely resonate with potential customers.

For instance, when I started exploring egg production in my poultry farming venture, I quickly realized that consumers were shifting toward healthier, organic options. This observation didn't just come from a marketing report; it stemmed from conversations with customers at local farmers' markets. They were looking for transparency in production and a commitment to sustainability. As a result, I adapted my farming practices and marketed my eggs as free-range and organic. This not only increased my sales but also built a loyal customer base that appreciated the ethical values behind my business.

In the broader context, understanding market needs can be the difference between thriving and merely surviving. Think of market needs as the bridge

connecting your passion to the demands of consumers. As entrepreneurs, it's essential to stay attuned to changes in consumer behavior, economic fluctuations, and industry trends. This means being proactive rather than reactive. Businesses that anticipate changes can pivot quickly, adjusting
their offerings to remain relevant. Whether you are in technology, retail, or agriculture, the principles remain the same: listen to your market, adapt, and innovate.

Identifying Customer Needs

Identifying customer needs is an extension of understanding the market. While market research provides a broad overview, digging deeper into customer needs helps you craft more personalized solutions. Think of your customers as partners in your entrepreneurial journey. Their feedback is a treasure trove of information that can guide your decision-making. To truly understand your customers, you must be willing to ask the right questions. What do they value? What are their pain points? Regular engagement with your audience can unveil insights that statistics alone cannot provide. Whether through social media, customer feedback forms, or direct communication, listening is key.

In my experience, I discovered that many consumers were overwhelmed by the plethora of options available to them. They craved clarity and simplicity in their choices. By providing educational resources, like guides on sustainable practices or tips on how to use my products, I not only addressed their needs but also positioned my brand as a trusted authority. This approach fosters loyalty and encourages repeat business.

Moreover, consider how your products or services fit into the broader context of your customers' lives. Are you meeting their emotional needs as well as their practical ones? For example, a business that sells health food products might not only focus on taste but also on promoting a lifestyle of wellness. By aligning your offerings with the values and aspirations of your customers, you create a more profound connection that can withstand market fluctuations.

Adapting To Changing Market Conditions

The ability to adapt to changing market conditions is one of the most critical skills an entrepreneur can develop. The business world is unpredictable, and external factors, such as economic downturns, technological advancements, and shifts in consumer behavior, can all impact your operations. Staying flexible and open-minded is essential for navigating these changes.

When the COVID-19 pandemic struck, many businesses faced unprecedented challenges. As a poultry farmer, I experienced significant disruptions in supply chains and a drop in demand from traditional markets. Instead of succumbing to despair, I embraced innovation. I shifted to online sales, utilizing social media to reach customers directly and promote my products. This pivot not only saved my business but also allowed me to build a stronger, more engaged community.

Adaptability is about more than just survival; it's about seizing opportunities that arise from change. For instance, consider how businesses that embraced e-commerce during the pandemic not only thrived but also expanded their customer base.

By recognizing the need for online solutions, they positioned themselves for future growth.

As entrepreneurs, we must also cultivate a mindset of resilience. Embrace failures as learning experiences rather than setbacks. Each challenge offers valuable lessons that can inform your strategy moving forward. Surround yourself with a support network of fellow entrepreneurs, mentors, and advisors who can offer insights and encouragement during tough times. Remember, the journey of entrepreneurship is not a straight path but a winding road filled with twists and turns. Those who navigate it successfully are the ones who remain agile and committed to learning.

Faith And Resilience In Business

At the core of my entrepreneurial journey lies a deep reliance on faith and resilience. These two elements are often interlinked, serving as a foundation that supports decision-making during uncertain times. As entrepreneurs, we face numerous challenges that can test our resolve. In those moments, faith becomes our anchor.

Faith, in this context, is not limited to religious beliefs alone but encompasses a broader trust in yourself, your vision, and your capacity to overcome obstacles. Drawing inspiration from biblical principles, I often reflect on passages that emphasize perseverance, such as *Romans 5:3-4*, which speaks to finding joy in tribulations, knowing they produce perseverance, character, and hope. This perspective has guided me through difficult moments, reminding me that every setback carries the potential for growth.Resilience is equally important. It's about bouncing back from failures and using those experiences to inform future decisions. Throughout my entrepreneurial journey, I've encountered challenges that have forced me to adapt and innovate. Rather than viewing failures as dead ends, I've learned to see them as stepping stones on the path to success.

As you embark on your entrepreneurial journey, cultivate a mindset of faith and resilience. Surround yourself with a community that shares your values and encourages your growth. Embrace the lessons that come from failures and setbacks, and let them inform your decisions moving forward.

Understanding market needs, identifying customer desires, adapting to changes, and fostering faith and resilience are the cornerstones of a successful entrepreneurial journey. Each principle is interconnected, forming a holistic approach to business that transcends industries. As you move forward, carry these insights with you, and remember that your journey is uniquely yours. By blending personal experiences with practical strategies, you can inspire others and create a meaningful impact in your chosen field.

Reflection Questions

→ **Understanding Market Needs**
- What are the top three market needs you've identified in your field? How did you discover them?
- How do you currently assess market trends, and what methods can you improve upon?

→ **Identifying Customer Needs**
- Think of a time when you misread a customer's needs. What did you learn from that experience?
- How can you implement customer feedback in your decision-making process moving forward?

→ **Adapting to Changing Market Conditions**
- Reflect on a recent change in your business environment. How did you respond, and what was the outcome?
- What strategies can you put in place to improve your business's adaptability to future changes?

→ **Faith and Resilience in Business**
- Describe a moment when your faith helped you navigate a challenging business situation. How did it change your perspective?
- What practices can you incorporate into your daily routine to strengthen your resilience?

Exercises

→ **Understanding Market Needs**
Market Trend Analysis: Choose a specific market trend relevant to your business. Research its background, current impact, and future predictions. Write a one-page summary detailing your findings and how they affect your business strategy.

→ **Identifying Customer Needs**
Customer Survey Creation: Design a short survey (5-10 questions) aimed at understanding your customers' needs better. Distribute it through your preferred channels and analyze the results to identify common themes.

→ **Adapting to Changing Market Conditions**
Scenario Planning: Create three hypothetical scenarios that could impact your business (e.g., a sudden market shift, a competitor's entry, changes in consumer preferences). For each scenario, outline potential responses and strategies to mitigate risks.

→ **Faith and Resilience in Business**
Gratitude Journal: Start a gratitude journal focused on your business journey. Write down at least three things you are grateful for each week, particularly during challenging times. Reflect on how these positive aspects can foster resilience.

Checklists

➜ **Understanding Market Needs Checklist**
  - ☐ Conduct a market analysis every quarter.
  - ☐ Identify and document at least three market trends.
  - ☐ Establish a system for tracking competitor activities.

➜ **Identifying Customer Needs Checklist**
  - ☐ Create and distribute a customer feedback survey.
  - ☐ Schedule regular check-ins with key customers for qualitative feedback. -Analyze feedback for act onable insights monthly.

➜ **Adapting to Changing Market Conditions Checklist**
  - ☐ Review and update your business plan biannually.
  - ☐ Ident fy key performance indicators (KPIs) that signal market changes. ☐ Develop a flexible action plan for responding to unexpected changes.

➜ **Faith and Resilience in Business Checklist**
  - ☐ Set aside time for daily reflection or prayer related to your business.
  - ☐ Create a support network of fellow entrepreneurs or mentors.
  - ☐ Regularly assess your business values and ensure alignment with your actions.

BUILDING STRONG CUSTOMER RELATIONSHIPS

For any entrepreneur, customer relationships are the lifeblood of a business. If I've learned one thing from my years in poultry farming, it's this: your customers are more than just buyers; they're part of a community that supports your vision and growth. The way you cultivate those relationships can make or break your success. And for me, faith has always been my guiding light in nurturing and sustaining those connections. When I first ventured into farming, I was focused mainly on the logistics, the product, the finances, the growth goals. I thought, "If I get these right, customers will naturally come." But soon, I found out that business wasn't that simple. Customers needed more than just high-quality eggs; they wanted trust, transparency, and to feel a sense of partnership in what I was building. Realizing that I had to focus on relationships wasn't just a business lesson; it became a spiritual one too, reminding me of the importance of humility, service, and integrity in all I do. And so I learned.

the heartbeat of any business whether you're farming, selling services, or launching a product, customers want to know the person behind the business. That is the first step to a healthy customer relationship. They want to trust that you understand their needs and will deliver on your promises. I remember one of my first loyal customers, a small restaurant owner. He'd come by regularly to pick up fresh eggs for his breakfast menu, and over time, we built a relationship beyond mere transactions.

There was one instance when I faced an unexpected drop in egg production. I dreaded letting this customer know because I knew how much he relied on my supply. When I fina ly called him, he appreciated the honesty anc transparency. Instead of losing a customer, I gained a supporter. He told me he respected my willingness to reach out and that he'd adjust his orders until I got back on track. That conversation reminded me that people value honesty, even when it means delivering tough news.

In every business, your relationship with customers should feel like a partnership. Trust is earned through the small but significant choices we make, like being transparent when things go sideways or taking an extra moment to check in on their needs. Customers remember these moments, and they can be the difference between a one-time sale and a loyal relationship.

Strategies For Building Relationships

There are countless ways to build strong relationships, but these three strategies have been essential to my journey in poultry farming and beyond:

→ **Consistency:**
Just as chickens expect food at the same time every day, customers expect reliable service. Consistency in quality, communication, and service builds trust. One of my clients once told me, "I know I can count on you, and that's rare." Even when things get busy or stressful, maintaining a steady standard speaks volumes about your commitment.

→ **Sincerity and Transparency:**
When I first started my farm, I made it a point to welcome customers to visit. I'd invite them

to see how the eggs were produced, talk about sustainable practices, and answer any questions they had. Those small visits fostered trust and allowed them to see I was genuinely invested in quality. This transparency didn't just build rapport; it built respect.

→ **Appreciation and Acknowledgment:** One of my favorite parts of running the farm is connecting with customers who appreciate the product and mission. I'd send a quick thank-you note to loyal customers or even throw in a small discount when I knew they'd had a particularly large order. Simple gestures like these go a long way in showing appreciation and making customers feel valued. They know you're not just seeing dollar signs but genuinely grateful for their support.

Listening To Your Customers

If there's one lesson my poultry farm has taught me, it's the importance of listening, just like you'd listen to a trusted friend. Customers, in their own way, will tell you exactly what they want if you're paying attention. I remember a time when I had to switch suppliers for my chicken feed. I noticed a slight dip in the quality of my eggs, and soon enough, a few regular customers commented on it. It wasn't a complaint, just a gentle observation.

rather than getting defensive, I took their feedback seriously and switched back to my original supplier. The results were immediate, and those customers noticed the difference. It was a lesson in humility, sometimes, the best business insights come directly from the people you're serving. Listening shows respect for their perspectives, and by acting on that feedback, you're demonstrating that you value them.

In my experience, being open to feedback and adjusting when necessary shows customers that they are a core part of your business. It's a simple yet powerful way to strengthen trust and build a relationship that goes beyond the transactional.

Excellent Service- Going Beyond The Sale

Excellent customer service is about providing more than just what you're selling; it's about creating an experience that reflects your values. My faith has always taught me the importance of service. When I approach customer interactions, I see it as a chance to serve them, just as I would serve my community or family.

For instance, early one morning, I got a call from a customer who needed an urgent egg order for a wedding event. My team and I scrambled to meet the request, even though it meant putting in extra hours and adjusting our orders. That customer became one of our most loyal supporters, referring others to my farm and even sending us a handwritten thank-you card. Going the extra mile can be tiring, but it's incredibly rewarding, and it's one of the best ways to show your commitment to customer service excellence. A few principles I live by for exceptional customer service:

→ **Empathy in Every Interaction:**
   Put yourself in their shoes. If a customer is

unhappy, try to understand their perspective rather than immediately jumping to a solution. Once, a customer received a batch of eggs that had been damaged during transport. Instead of a simple replacement, I included a small discount and a note of apology. That extra touch showed empathy, and they appreciated it enough to stick with my business.

→ **Prompt Communication:**
Customers expect timely responses, especially in today's social media world. A quick response can make customers feel valued, while delays often lead to frustration. Even if I can't resolve the issue right away, a message letting them know I'm on it goes a long way.

→ **Following Through:**
If I promise to check on something, I make sure to get back to them. Over time, people know they can count on you, and that builds a foundation of trust that every successful relationship requires.

Engaging With Your Community

One of the most rewarding parts of running my farm has been the sense of community that's developed around it. Engaging with the community isn't just about networking; it's about shared values and creating a circle of support. My poultry farm hosts workshops on sustainable farming practices, where customers and local families can see firsthand how we operate. These events create a sense of transparency and give customers a reason to feel connected to the farm beyond the product they buy. Faith has taught me that community is everything; when we're all working together, we're stronger than when we're on our own. Participating in local events, donating produce, and volunteering time helps reinforce my commitment to serving not only my customers but the entire community. When customers see this, they feel a sense of pr de in supporting a business that cares about something beyond profit.

Relationships are the foundation of success building strong customer relationships is essential for long-term success. Each interaction, each small gesture of kindness, and each effort to serve with integrity builds the foundation of trust. Just as I care for my chickens day in and day out, I invest the same care into relationships with my customers.

Being an entrepreneur, especially one driven by faith, means striving to serve people genuinely. Customers remember the way you make them feel, and each interaction is an opportunity to embody the principles that ground your business.

As we move forward, remember that building these connections is both an art and a discipline. Keep your values close, listen to your customers, and be unafraid to invest time and care into each relationship. In the end, it's not just about business; it's about serving with heart and faith.

Reflection Questions

→ **Current Practices Assessment:**
What methods are you currently using to build
customer relationships? List them out and
evaluate their effectiveness.

→ **Trust and Loyalty:**
How do you currently cultivate trust with your
customers? Can you identify specific actions
that have led to increased loyalty?

→ **Personalization:**
In what ways are you personalizing your
customer interactions? Are there opportunities
for further customization that you might be
missing?

→ **Feedback Mechanisms:**
How do you collect feedback from your
customers? Are there any patterns or insights
you've noticed from this feedback?

→ **Community Engagement:**
How involved is your business in the local
community? What partnerships or collaborations
have you established that enhance customer
connections?

Practical Exercises

→ **Customer Relationship Audit:**
Take one day to observe your customer interactions. Note down key moments where you engage with customers and reflect on the outcomes. What worked well? What didn't? Use these insights to identify areas for improvement.

→ **Feedback Session:**
Organize a feedback session with your team. Share customer feedback and brainstorm actionable steps to address any concerns or suggestions raised by customers.

→ **Personalization Plan:**
Develop a plan to enhance personalization in your customer interactions. Choose one area of your business (e.g., email marketing, customer service) and outline specific steps to make it more personalized.

→ **Community Engagement Brainstorm:**
Create a list of potential community engagement opportunities. Identify local events, charities, or partnerships that align with your brand values and could enhance your connection with customers.

→ **Role-Playing Scenarios:**
Conduct role-playing exercises with your team to practice active listening and exceptional customer service. Use real-world scenarios to simulate customer interactions and develop effective responses.

Checklist For Immediate Application

Actionable Steps to Enhance Customer Relationships

→ **Evaluate Current Practices:**
  - ☐ List your current customer relationship strategies and assess their effectiveness.

→ **Enhance Personalization**
  - ☐ Identify three ways to personalize customer interactions within your business. Implement at least one immediately.

→ **Implement Feedback Channels:**
  - ☐ Set up or improve feedback mechanisms (e.g., surveys, suggestion boxes) to gather customer insights regularly.

→ **Train Your Team:**
  - ☐ Organize a training session focused on active listening and exceptional customer service techniques for all team members.

→ **Establish Community Partnerships:**
  - ☐ Research and identify at least two local organizations or events where your business can engage and build relationships.

→ **Create a Customer Engagement Calendar:**
  - ☐ Develop a monthly calendar outlining key customer engagement activities (e.g., social media posts,

community events) to keep your
efforts organized and consistent.

→ **Review Customer Service Protocols:**
  ☐ Analyze your current customer service
  protocols. Are they effective? If not,
  outline adjustments that could lead to
  improved service.

→ **Follow Up with Customers:**
  ☐ Choose three recent customers to follow
  up with. Ask for their feedback on their
  experience and express your
  appreciation for their bus ness.

→ **Celebrate Customer Milestones:**
  ☐ Identify ways to acknowledge and
  celebrate important customer milestones
  (e.g., anniversaries, birthdays) to
  strengthen your relationship.

→ **Monitor and Adjust:**
  ☐ Set up a regular review process to
  assess the effectiveness of your
  customer relationship strategies and
  make adjustments based on
  feedback and results.

EFFECTIVE MARKETING STRATEGIES

When I first started out in poultry farming, I'll be honest, "marketing" felt like a foreign concept. I was focused on producing quality eggs, getting my operations streamlined, and building a customer base. I thought, "If the product is good enough, people will come, right?" Well, not quite. The early days taught me that quality alone doesn't automatically get you noticed. It's the story behind the product, the value you offer, and how you communicate it that brings people in.

For any entrepreneur, whether you're selling eggs or launching a tech startup, effective marketing isn't just a side activity; it's the bridge between your product and your audience. Marketing is about understanding who your customers are, what matters to them, and crafting messages that resonate.

Over time, I learned that, like farming, marketing is both art and science. Here's what I've discovered along the way.

Continue To Know Your Audience

Before you can reach customers, you need to know who they are. This sounds simple, but understanding your market is one of the most overlooked steps in marketing. I've learned that the more specific you can be about who you're serving, the more effective your marketing will be. Early in my farming journey, I thought my eggs would appeal to everyone. But as I grew, I noticed patterns, my most loyal distributors were people who found something appealing in my sales experiences. Sometimes the eggs would be smaller in size but they would indulge me and still purchase. To connect with these groups, I had to dig deeper into their needs and motivations. I found out that regardless of my farm being far out from the city. They would come knowing that I give out 2 extra crates to cover up for the long distance. Some also wanted assurance of quality and safety. My marketing changed as I started speaking directly to those needs I observed. I would always explain how we prioritize quality and care. Understancing your market allows you to be intentional in how you communicate and makes your message far more relatable

Crafting Your Brand Message

As a faith-driven entrepreneur, I see storytelling as more than just a technique; it's a way to connect with people on a personal level. When I tell the story of my farm, the values behind it, the struggles, and the small victories, I'm giving customers something to believe in. People aren't just buying eggs; they're supporting a vision and a mission. Think of your brand message as the "why" behind your business.

One day, I decided to share the story of a tough season I'd gone through on the farm. Production had dropped, costs were high, and I was feeling stretched thin. But I held on, grounded n my faith and commitment. Sharing that journey, along with my commitment to quality and resilience, made an impression on customers. They felt connected to the farm, and many told me later that they kept buying from us because they believed in what we were doing. When crafting your brand message, think about what makes your journey unique. Why did you start this business? What values do you bring? Whether it's your dedication to quality, passion for sustainability, or commitment to serving, find a way to share that story with customers. It doesn't have to be flashy, sometimes, sincerity speaks louder than the most polished branding.

Going Where Your Customers Are

In today's world, digital marketing is indispensable. Early on, I underestimated the power of digital platforms. I figured that since I was running a farm, it would be enough to build word-of-mouth connections. But I quickly learned that online presence could amplify my reach in ways that traditional methods couldn't.

For my farm, social media became a game-changer. I started sharing photos of the farm, updates on production, and little snippets of farm life. I realized that people loved to see the "behind-the-scenes" of where their food came from. Social media helped humanize the business and built a community around it. Here are a few digital essentials that can help any entrepreneur build an online presence:

→ **Website**:
Your website is your digital storefront. Make it user-friendly, informative, and visually appealing. A clear layout, easy navigation, and concise information about your product can make all the difference
.

→ **Social Media:**
Pick one or two platforms where your target customers are likely to be. Post regularly, interact with followers, and share stories that

reflect your values and business journey. For me, Instagram and Facebook became great platforms for sharing farm life, educating followers on sustainability, and engaging with customers.

→ **Email Marketing:**
Collecting emails from customers or website visitors lets you keep in touch, share updates, and offer special deals. It was tough at first getting people to subscribe to the newsletter. But after a while. More people took the time to do that. The newsletters highlight what's happening on the farm, new products, and sometimes just a quick note of gratitude to my loyal customers. It keeps me connected to them in a more personal way.

→ **Content Marketing:**
Write blogs, record videos, or share tips related to your field. As a farmer, I started a blog to discuss sustainable farming, poultry care, and even some recipes for egg-based dishes Content marketing establishes you as an expert in your field and draws in people interested in your insights.

→ **Search Engine Optimization (SEO):**
It is about making your business visible to potential customers actively searching for solutions you provide. A solid SEO strategy can boost your online visibility and drive organic traffic to your website. But don't stop there; engage with your audience through social media. It's a platform where you can share your brand story, connect with

customers, and create a community around your business.

Offline Marketing Techniques (Old School, but Effective)

While digital marketing is essential, offline strategies still have a unique impact, especially when building local loyalty. For my farm, community events and partnerships have been invaluable. By participating in farmers' markets, collaborating with local businesses, and hosting farm tours, I made face-to-face connections with customers. There's something irreplaceable about shaking hands, having a conversation, and letting people experience the business firsthand.

→ **Networking Events and Trade Shows:**
Even if your business isn't food-related, attending industry events helps build credibility and spreads your name. Being visible in the local community builds trust and often brings in referrals.

→ **Collaborations and Partnerships:**
Teaming up with businesses that share similar values amplifies your reach. For instance, I partnered with a local health food store to provide fresh eggs and co-hosted events focused on healthy eating. Partnerships like these build credibility and introduce your brand to a wider audience.

→ **Flyers and Local Ads:**
Sometimes, a well-placed flyer at a popular stop, High traffic stores, café or community center can bring in more interest than a

Facebook ad. It's a more targeted approach for local businesses and connects with people in your immediate area.

Leveraging Community Engagement

For me, engaging with the community isn't just a marketing strategy; it's a chance to give back. Supporting your community builds goodwill, establishes trust, and creates a loyal customer base. I've found that engaging with the community creates a circle of support around my farm, and those relationships are invaluable during challenging times. One year, we had a bad season that affected production. I was worried about losing customers, but to my surprise, many offered support, some even volunteering to do what they could. That kind of loyalty isn't built overnight. It comes from investing time, sharing knowledge, and genuinely being there for the community. Whether it's sponsoring a local event, volunteering, or donating products to a charity, there are many ways to make an impact.

Final Thoughts

Marketing is more than just pushing a product. It's about building connections, sharing values, and creating an experience that resonates. For me, marketing has become an extension of my faith journey, a chance to serve others, uplift my community, and share the values that guide my life and business.

Effective marketing strategies come from the heart. When you approach marketing as a way to give, to share, and to connect, it becomes less of a chore and more of a fulfilling part of your journey. Whether online or offline, let your values shine through in every interaction.

People remember businesses that make them feel valued, and when you put care and authenticity at the center of your strategy, it reflects in the relationships you build and the loyalty you earn. Just like tending to chickens, marketing takes patience, consistency, and genuine effort. The seeds you plant today will bear fruit tomorrow. So, go out there, share your story, engage with your community, and let your light shine, your customers will thank you for it.

Reflection Questions and Exercises

Questions for Evaluating Current Marketing
Strategies

→ **What marketing channels are you
currently using?**
Take a moment to list all the channels you
utilize, such as social media, email, print, or
events. How effective have they been in
reaching your target audience?

→ **Who is your target audience?**
Describe your ideal customer. Have you
considered their demographics, interests,
and pain points? Are you tailoring your
messaging to meet their needs?

→ **What is your brand message?**
Reflect on your brand story. Does it resonate
with your audience? Are your values clearly
communicated across all platforms?

→ **How do you measure success?**
Consider the metrics you use to evaluate the
effectiveness of your marketing strategies.
Are you tracking engagement, conversions,
or customer feedback?

→ **What feedback have you received from
customers?**
Gather insights from customer feedback.
How can you incorporate this feedback into
your marketing strategies for improvement?

Practical Exercises

➜ **Conduct a Marketing Audit:**
Take a day to assess your current marketing strategies. Review each channel and evaluate its effectiveness based on specific metrics. What's working, and what needs adjustment?

➜ **Create Customer Personas:**
Develop detailed profiles for your ideal customers. Include their demographics, interests, challenges, and motivations. Use this information to tailor your marketing messages.

➜ **Craft Your Brand Story:**
Spend time writing or revising your brand story. Make it authentic and relatable. Test it out on friends or colleagues to see if it resonates with them.

➜ **Experiment with New Channels:**
Choose one new marketing channel or technique to try over the next month. It could be a different social media platform, an email marketing campaign, or hosting a local event.

➜ **Gather and Analyze Feedback:**
Create a simple survey or feedback form to share with your customers. Ask them about their experiences with your brand and how you can improve.

Checklist to Enhance Your Marketing Strategy

→ **Conduct a Marketing Audit**
- ☐ Review all current marketing channels and campaigns.
- ☐ Analyze the performance metrics of each channel.
- ☐ Identify strengths and weaknesses in your marketing strategy.

→ **Define Your Target Audience**
- ☐ Create detailed customer personas based on demographics, interests, and behaviors.
- ☐ Ensure you understand their pain points and needs.
- ☐ Reassess your audience regularly to adapt to changes.

→ **Refine Your Brand Message**
- ☐ Write a clear and compelling brand story.
- ☐ Ensure your messaging aligns with customer values.
- ☐ Test your brand message with trusted individuals for feedback.

→ **Set SMART Marketing Goals**
- ☐ Define specific, measurable, achievable, relevant, and time-bound (SMART) goals.
- ☐ Prioritize goals based on your business objectives.
- ☐ Create a timeline for achieving each

goal.

→ **Utilize Digital Marketing Tools**
- ☐ Research and implement tools for SEO, social media management, and email marketing.
- ☐ Use analytics tools to track website traffic and engagement metrics.
- ☐ Automate repetitive tasks where possible to save time. (Use Zapier or Make.com)

→ **Engage with Your Audience**
- ☐ Develop a social media engagement plan.
- ☐ Respond promptly to comments, messages, and reviews.
- ☐ Create opportunities for audience interaction, such as polls or Q&A sessions.

→ **Experiment with New Tactics**
- ☐ Identify one new marketing tactic to implement each month.
- ☐ Monitor the performance of new strategies closely.
- ☐ Be flexible and ready to pivot based on results.

→ **Gather Customer Feedback**
- ☐ Create surveys or feedback forms to solicit input from customers.
- ☐ Analyze feedback for actionable insights.
- ☐ Implement changes based on feedback received.

➜ **Leverage Community Involvement**
- ☐ Identify local events or organizations to partner with.
- ☐ Engage in community service or sponsorship opportunities.
- ☐ Promote community involvement through your marketing channels.

➜ **Review and Adjust Regularly**
- ☐ Schedule regular check-ins to assess your marketing strategy.
- ☐ Be prepared to make adjustments based on market trends and feedback.
- ☐ Celebrate successes and learn from challenges.

FINANCIAL MANAGEMENT FOR GROWTH

During the initial start up in poultry, I had a basic understanding of finances, this was all from the previous failed businesses in the past. But they were enough to know I needed to watch my costs and keep track of my sales. But as my business grew, I quickly realized that financial management is about so much more than just breaking even. It's about planning for growth, being prepared for the unexpected, and always knowing where you stand financially. This isn't just a chapter on managing money; it's a lesson in staying grounded, making wise choices, and building a foundation for a sustainable future.

In my farming journey, I learned firsthand that successful financial management is both an art and a science. Here's a closer look at the financial strategies I developed, often through trial and error, and always rooted in faith that the resources I had were there for a reason.

Starting with a Plan

I remember when I first drafted my farm's budget. It was a simple list of expenses, feed, equipment, and general upkeep. I didn't fully appreciate the importance of budgeting until I faced my first financial crunch. Suddenly, every penny mattered, and I realized how crucial it was to allocate resources wisely. A solid budget isn't just about listing costs; it's a roadmap that helps you steer your business in the right direction.

Budgeting has become the cornerstone of my financial strategy. Every quarter, I sit down, review my expenses, adjust where necessary, and make sure my spending aligns with my goals. Here are a few budgeting essentials that have kept me on track:

→ **Separate Needs from Wants:**
In the beginning, I found myself wanting to invest in the latest equipment or expand sooner than planned. But financial discipline taught me to focus on essentials first, making sure the core elements of my business were steady before expanding.

→ **Account for Seasonal Variations:**
With farming, seasons impact everything from feed costs to demand. I learned to budget with these fluctuations in mind, setting aside extra funds during high-revenue months to cover leaner times. This principle applies to any business, anticipate slow periods and plan accordingly.

→ **Stay Flexible, but Set Boundaries**:
Life has a way of throwing unexpected expenses into the mix. Early on, I'd sometimes spend on impulse if I thought it would improve operations. But I learned to approach each spending decision with discernment. If an expense didn't align with my long-term goals, it didn't make the cut.

Keeping the Lifeblood Flowing

In the world of business, cash flow is king. While profits show the big picture, cash flow shows your business's day-to-day health. I've learned that even a profitable business can struggle if cash flow is mismanaged. There were times I had significant accounts receivable, but without cash on hand, it felt like I was paddling upstream.

To understand cash flow, I had to look beyond the simple inflows and outflows. I needed to know where my money was tied up, how long it took to convert products into revenue, and what options were available if cash ran low. A few key lessons that transformed my cash flow management include:

→ **Shorten the Receivables Cycle:**
At one point, I was letting certain clients take longer than necessary to pay. I started encouraging quicker payment terms, offering small discounts for early payment, which helped stabilize cash flow.

→ **Separate Personal and Business Finances:**
This one is huge. When I first started, it was tempting to dip into business funds for personal needs, especially when cash was tight. But keeping finances separate helps maintain clarity and accountability, which are crucial when making strategic decisions.

→ **Know Your Funding Options:**
Funding isn't just for startups. Whether it's taking out a small loan to cover an unexpected expense or finding investors for expansion, funding can give a business the boost it needs at the right time. But be wise, funding is only beneficial if it aligns with your

growth plan and financial goals.

Gaining Insights from Numbers

Financial analysis can sound daunting, but it's one of the best ways to understand your business's true performance. As a business analyst, this was easy for me. working with spreadsheets and metrics. For entrepreneurs, you can take a crash course on Youtube or Udemy if you have the time. or you can also hire a financial analysis to do it for you.

The huge impact it had on my decisions. Just like tracking growth metrics on the farm, analyzing financial health gives you a snapshot of where you are and where you're headed. These are the key tools that helped me manage growth:

→ **Profit and Loss Statements (P&L):**
   This is your business's "report card." It shows how much revenue you've brought in, what your expenses were, and your bottom line. Reviewing my P&L every month helped me identify areas to cut back anc spot trends over time.

→ **Cash Flow Statements:**
   This statement shows where your money comes from and where it goes. It's a real eye-opener for understanding if you're generating enough cash from operations or relying too heavily on outside sources.

→ **Break-even Analysis:**
   This tool helps determine the point at which revenue covers all expenses. In my early days, knowing my break-even point gave me

peace of mind. It reassured me that if I sold a certain amount, I'd stay afloat, even during challenging months.

Financial Prudence

While running a business requires financial acumen, my faith plays a significant role in how I approach growth. There were seasons where, despite all my planning, finances didn't look promising. In those moments, I leaned on faith, reminding myself that my work was part of a bigger purpose. This perspective has taught me to balance prudence with trust.

When I was faced with a big decision, like expanding my farm or investing in a new line of products, I'd take a step back. I'd pray for guidance, seek counsel, and ask myself: Is this in alignment with my mission? Over time, I've learned that faith is as much a guiding principle as a financial strategy.

Practical Tips for Financial Growth

Growing a business requires balancing my ambition with practicality. Here are some hands-on strategies I've developed over time:

→ **Prioritize Saving for Reinvestment:**
It's tempting to use every bit of profit, but setting aside a portion for reinvestment ensures you're always prepared for new opportunities and growth.

→ **Automate Payments**:
I automated routine expenses like feed

44

purchases, payroll, and utilities. It saved time and ensured that I was never late on essential payments.

→ **Monitor Your Debt Levels:**
IF and ONLY IF you decide to take on debt for growth, monitor it closely. Always calculate your ability to pay it back without sacrificing operational cash flow.

Lessons from the Farm

There's a proverb that says, "Consider the ant, consider its ways and be wise." I used to think it only applied to hard work, but now I see it also speaks to planning and resourcefulness. Just like the ant prepares for the future, financial wisdom means looking beyond today.

One of the toughest financial lessons I learned was in the early stages of my farm. I'd experienced a strong initial demand, and my natural reaction was to expand. But, in my eagerness, I overlooked cash flow constraints, and soon, I was struggling to cover operational costs. That season taught me that growth requires not only faith but also patience and caution. Since then, I've approached every growth decision with the mindset of a farmer, tending to each new venture with care, knowing that good things take time.

Financial management is a journey

It isn't a one-time thing, it's a journey, just like any other aspect of business. It requires ongoing attention, reflection, and adjustment. Sometimes, it's about making tough choices, and sometimes, it's about having faith that things will work out.

As entrepreneurs, our approach to finances says a lot about our mindset. Are we rooted in purpose? Are we operating from a place of abundance or scarcity? Money isn't just a means to an end; it's a resource that, when managed well, allows us to build, to serve, and to give back. And just like in farming, the seeds we plant financially today set the stage for tomorrow's harvest.

Whether you're balancing a budget, planning your next big move, or weathering a financial storm, remember this: a solid financial foundation is built on wise decisions, faithful stewardship, and resilience. By making each financial choice count, you're not just securing your business; you're also planting seeds for a future that reflects your values, your purpose, and your unwavering faith.

Reflection Questions and Exercises

Reflection Questions

➡ What are your current practices for budgeting and tracking expenses?

➡ How often do you review your cash flow, and what insights have you gained?

➡ Which funding options have you explored, and what barriers have you encountered?

➡ What financial analysis tools do you currently use, and how effective are they for your business?

Practical Exercises

➡ Create a detailed budget for the next quarter, outlining projected income and expenses.

➡ Monitor your cash flow weekly for a month, noting any patterns or issues that arise.

➡ Research three different funding options available to you and outline the pros and cons of each.

➡ Choose a financial analysis tool to implement, and track key metrics over the next month.

Checklist for Immediate Application

→ **Conduct a Financial Audit**
- ☐ Review current budgets, cash flow, and financial statements.

→ **Establish a Budget**
- ☐ Create a realistic budget for the next fiscal year.

→ **Monitor Cash Flow**
- ☐ Set up a system for tracking daily cash inflows and outflows.

→ **Explore Funding Options**
- ☐ Research at least three funding sources and evaluate their suitability.

→ **Implement Financial Analysis Tools**
- ☐ Choose and implement one financial analysis tool.

→ **Set Up Regular Reviews**
- ☐ Schedule monthly reviews of your financial performance.

→ **Seek Professional Advice**
- ☐ Consider consulting with a financial advisor or accountant.

LEADERSHIP AND TEAM BUILDING

Becoming a leader wasn't something I consciously planned. When you decide to start a business. It is one of the roles you have to fill. When I started my poultry farm, it was just me, a few birds one farm help and the open field where we later began crop farming. But as the business grew, so did the need for a team to help me keep things running smoothly. I soon realized that leading others wasn't just about delegating tasks; it was about inspiring, guiding, upholding your policies, and building something meaningful together. My journey into leadership taught me that true leadership comes from serving, lifting others, and leading by example.

This chapter dives into my journey with leadership and team building, illustrating how my fa th, resilience, ard a commitment to giving value shaped my approach. I learned to grow as a leader, nurture my team, ard foster a workplace culture that empowers everyone involved.

Learning To Lead From The Heart

Leadership starts from within. I remember those early days when I was overwhelmed by the idea of leading others. my initial thought was, "how can i lead when i'm still learning myself?" but I quickly learned that leadership is about the journey, not perfection. It's about having a vision making decisions based on that vision, and being willing to grow along the way. the best leaders are lifelong learners, and here's how i developed my leadership skills:

→ **Start with Self-Awareness:** The first step to leadership is understanding yourself. I had to recognize my strengths, like decision-making and communication, but also my weaknesses. Knowing where I struggled helped me focus on improving in those areas and being transparent with my team.

→ **Lead by Example:** I've always believed that actions speak louder than words. On the farm, I didn't just tell my team what needed to be done; I showed them. Whether it meant assisting them with the work however way I can during early morning shifts or staying late to ensure things were done right, I aimed to model the behavior I expected from others.

→ **Embrace Humility:** Leadership isn't about always being right; it's about being willing to listen, learn, and adapt. One humbling experience was when a team member suggested a new, more efficient feeding method. Initially, I resisted the change, but after seeing the positive results, I realized that leadership also means being open to others' insights.

Finding People Who Share Your Vision

Building a successful team isn't just about hiring skilled individuals; it's about finding people who resonate with your vision and values. My faith taught me the importance of unity, and I believe that a strong team is built on shared beliefs and a common purpose. When I first started hiring, I looked for individuals who shared a genuine passion for farming, their lifestyle also aligned with the farm lifestyle and who were committed to excellence. here's what i've learned about team-building over the years:

→ **Hire for Character and Attitude, Not Just Skills:**
Skills can be taught, but character is intrinsic. I've found that people with integrity, dedication, and a positive attitude are the backbone of a successful team. They may make mistakes but they will learn from them and do better. I remember h ring one of my current farm managers not based on his experience but his genuine enthusiasm for farming. He grew up in the Northern region of Nigeria where Agriculture is what they do best.

→ **Encourage Collaboration and Communication:**
A strong team is built on trust and open communication. I make it a point to hold regular team meetings where everyone has a chance to share ideas, concerns, and progress. By fostering an environment of open dialogue, I've seen my team become more cohesive and committed.

→ **Delegate with Trust:**
Early on, I struggled with letting go of control, but I soon learned that effective delegation builds trust and allows others to grow. I gradually started entrusting my team with more responsibilities, empowering them to make decisions in their areas of expertise.

Fostering A Positive Work Culture

A positive work culture doesn't happen by accident; it's cultivated through intentional practices and a shared commitment to respect, empathy, and encouragement. I wanted my farm to be a place where everyone felt valued, where their efforts were appreciated, and where they could grow both personally and professionally.
My approach to work culture focuses on fostering kindness, respect, and community. Here's how I brought these principles into my business:

→ **Celebrate Successes, Big and Small:**
One of the simplest ways to boost morale is by celebrating achievements. Whether it's a milestone in production or a team member's personal success, I make sure to acknowledge and celebrate each one.

→ **Encourage Work-Life Balance:**
Farming can be demanding, but I remind my team of the importance of rest and balance. I provided flexible hours when possible, and encouraged my team to prioritize their well-being.

→ **Create a Safe and Inclusive Environment:**
Respect is the foundation of a positive work culture. I make it clear that every team member's voice matters. When conflicts arise, I address them directly, ensuring that everyone feels heard and respected.

Conflict Resolution And Management

Conflict is inevitable in any workplace, but it doesn't have to be negative. I used to shy away from conflict, hoping it would resolve itself, but I learned that addressing issues directly leads to stronger relationships and a healthier work environment. Today, I view conflict as an opportunity for growth and understanding. these are a few of my strategies for managing conflict effectively:

→ **Address Issues Early and Openly:**
If I sense tension or conflict brewing, I don't wait for it to escalate. I initiate a private, respectful conversation to understand each person's perspective and work toward a resolution.

→ **Seek Understanding, Not Blame:**
During a conflict, it's easy to assign blame. However, I've learned to approach these situations with empathy, focusing on understanding everyone's perspective. This approach fosters mutual respect and encourages solutions that benef t everyone involved.

→ **Encourage Resolution through Dialogue:**
I promote open dialogue, encouraging team members to discuss their concerns directly. I often serve as a mediator, guiding the conversation toward understanding and resolution rather than focusing on the problem alone.

Leadership Through Service

One of the most valuable leadership lessons came during a challenging season on the farm. We had an unexpected poultry disease outbreak that required long hours, quick thinking, and difficult decisions. Instead of directing from a distance, I worked side-by-side with my team, from early morning treatments to late-night clean-ups. We pulled through that season, not just because of hard work but because we stood united, with each person contributing their unique strengths.

I realized leadership isn't about commanding; it's about serving. When I showed my team that I was willing to do the hard work alongside them, it reinforced our bond and inspired them to take ownership of their roles.

Practical Tips For Building A Resilient Team

Here are some hands-on strategies that have been invaluable in building and maintaining my team:

→ **Establish Clear Roles and Responsibilities:**
   Each team member should know their role and how it contributes to the business. Defining responsibilities reduces confusion and enhances productivity.

→ **Provide Opportunities for Growth:**
   Whether through training, workshops, or new projects, I offer my team opportunities to learn and grow. A motivated team is a productive team, and growth inspires

commitment. Foster Team Spirit through Regular Check-ins: I conduct regular one-on-one meetings to discuss each team member's goals, challenges, and feedback. These sessions build trust, showing my team that I'm invested in their success.

Leadership Grounded In Faith And Purpose

Leading a team is one of the most rewarding yet challenging parts of running a business. It demands patience, wisdom, and a constant willingness to learn. Every team dynamic is different, and what works for one team may not work for another. but with a foundation of respect, empathy, and faith, I've found that leadership becomes less about controlling outcomes and more about cultivating potential.

I've come to view leadership as a calling, an opportunity to serve others while working toward a shared vision. Through this journey, I've learned that the strength of my team is one of my greatest assets. When the farm thrives, it's not just because of my efforts; it's a testament to the hard work, dedication, and shared commitment of every individual involved.

Leadership isn't about having all the answers; it's about guiding others toward a common purpose, inspiring them to become the best versions of themselves. and working together to build something meaningful. Whether you're a seasoned entrepreneur or just starting out, remember that effective leadership is rooted in service, empathy, and a genuine desire to make a difference. The lessons I've learned as a leader have shaped not only my business but also my character. By leading with purpose, humility, and faith, I've seen the profound impact that one person's vision can have when it becomes a shared journey.

Reflection Questions And Exercises

Reflection Questions

→ What qualities do you believe are essential for effective leadership in your context?

→ How do you currently support the development of your team members?

→ What steps can you take to improve your communication skills?

→ How do you handle conflicts within your team, and what could you do differently?

Practical Exercises

→ Create a personal development plan that outlines specific leadership skills you want to develop.

→ Organize a team-building activity that encourages collaboration and relationship-building.

→ Schedule one-on-one meetings with team members to understand their aspirations and concerns.

→ Conduct a team survey to gather feedback on workplace culture and areas for improvement.

Checklist For Immediate Application

→ **Assess Leadership Skills**
   ☐ Identify areas for improvement in your leadership approach.

→ **Enhance Communication**
   ☐ Implement regular team check-ins and feedback sessions.

→ **Invest in Team Development**
   ☐ Plan a training session or workshop to enhance team skills.

SUSTAINABILITY AND SOCIAL RESPONSIBILITY

In the early days of building my farm, I didn't fully understand what it meant to be sustainable or socially responsible. I thought success depended solely on financial growth and productivity. However, as I continued working closely with the land and our community, I started seeing the bigger picture.

Running a business means understanding that every decision we make has consequences, not just for our bottom line, but for the environment, our employees, and our community. I realized that to truly build something lasting, sustainability and social responsibility had to become core parts of our mission.

In this chapter, we'll explore how a sustainable and socially responsible business approach can deepen your business's roots, grow trust with customers, and create a positive impact on the world. Together, we'll walk through essential sustainable practices, explore how to engage and involve stakeholders, and learn how to measure our social and environmental impact.

The Foundation of Responsible Business

Sustainability, at its heart, means creating a business that doesn't just survive but endures and thrives in a way that preserves resources for the future. For a farm, sustainability means nurturing the soil, water, and air so they remain healthy for future crops. But in business, sustainability involves everything from mindful resource management to fair labor practices. I found that taking a sustainable approach doesn't just benefit the environment, it also builds a stronger, more resilient business. It creates room for seamless continuity

My journey into sustainability started with simple changes: instead of relying on synthetic fertilizers, I began composting and rotating crops to keep the soil fertile naturally. These small shifts led to healthier crops, lower costs, and a deeper connection to the land. Sustainability isn't about massive, costly changes; it's about intentional, practical choices that build a foundation for long-term growth. Here's how any business, big or small, can start incorporating sustainable practices:

→ **Optimize Resource Use**:
Review every step of your operations to find areas where materials might be used more efficiently. On the farm, we use the poultry waste for manure, which translates to lower bills and more sustainable operational flow. Reduce Business Waste: Every business generates waste. Look at it as anything or any idea that the business can not fully utilize for itself. Especially after analysis but by assessing where it occurs, we can make impactful changes. Some are outdated practices and processes that become less effective, outdated skills, redundant roles.

→ **Seek Renewable Resources:**
Transitioning to renewable energy sources is a powerful step toward sustainability. Investing in solar energy for part of our farm's power needs,

for example, helped us reduce our energy costs while relying less on non-renewable resources.

Sustainable Practices in Business

Sustainable practices aren't limited to environmental changes, they include policies and practices that ensure long-term value and responsible growth for your business. Adopting these practices, whether on a farm or in an office, demonstrates a commitment to integrity and conscientious leadership. Here are some practical steps to get started:

→ **Implement Circular Practices:**
   This is repurposing resources for continuity. On the farm, we recycled plant waste back into the soil as compost. For other businesses, this means using recycled materials.

→ **Embrace Ethical Sourcing:**
   It's vital to know where your materials or products are coming from and to support suppliers who follow fair labor and sustainable practices. In farming, sourcing seeds and materials from ethical suppliers ensured quality of yield .

→ **Assess Your Supply Chain:**
   As I grew more aware of sustainability, I began to streamline our supply chain, cutting out unnecessary steps that created waste or pollution. This not only reduced costs but also

made our processes more efficient and environmentally friendly.

Making a Positive Impact in the Community

Social responsibility is about positively impacting the people and communities you touch. From hiring practices to community involvement.

"Social responsibility begins with a genuine desire to uplift and support those around you."

As my farm grew, I made it a priority to support our local community by hiring locally, providing training, and sourcing supplies from nearby businesses. This didn't just strengthen our ties to the community; it also boosted our reputation and brought in loyal customers who valued our commitment to local growth. Some ways businesses can make a social impact include:

→ **Support Local Employment:**
   Employing people from the community not only strengthens local economies but builds a reliable, loyal workforce that understands the business's unique needs and values.

→ **Engage in Community Programs:**
   Offer volunteer days, sponsor local events, or support nearby schools and nonprofits. For instance, my team and I began hosting free agricultural workshops for young people

interested in farming, sharing our skills and creating opportunities.

→ **Promote Fair Labor Practices:**
Treating employees with respect and fairness, offering competitive wages, and providing growth opportunities not only create a positive work environment but also boost productivity and morale.

Building Trust and Shared Values

Stakeholders, customers, employees, investors, and even your community, have a vested interest in the way you run your business. Engaging them in your sustainability and social responsibility efforts builds trust and helps you gain a deeper understanding of their expectations and values. By being transparent about your goals and initiatives, you can inspire stakeholders to support your mission and become ambassadors for your business. Some effective ways to engage stakeholders include:

→ **Open Communication:**
Regularly share your progress and goals with stakeholders. Transparency not only builds trust but also invites them to offer valuable insights and support.

→ **Customer Involvement:**
Customers appreciate businesses that operate

with integrity. Find ways to engage them, whether by offering eco-friendly product options or explaining the steps you're taking to improve sustainability.

→ **Employee Engagement:**
When I introduced sustainable practices on the farm, I asked for my team's feedback and suggestions Their ideas were invaluable, and their involvement helped create a culture of ownership and commitment.

Tracking Progress and Refining Goals

Setting sustainability goals is only the first step; measuring progress and making necessary adjustments are what tru y drive impact. On the farm, I tracked data like water usage, crop yields, and waste production to see if our sustainability efforts were yielding results. Regular tracking helped me refine our practices, identify what worked, and make informed changes. Here's how you can effectively measure impact:

→ **Set Clear, Measurable Goals:**
Define what success looks like for each initiative, whether it's reducing waste by a certain percentage or increasing local hires. Clear goals make it easier to track progress and see the tangible effects of your efforts.

→ **Regularly Review and Report Progress:**
Reporting on sustainability efforts, whether

through an annual report or a newsletter, keeps stakeholders informed and demonstrates accountability.

→ **Continuously Improve Based on Results:** Sustainability is an ongoing process. Use data from your impact measurements to refine your practices and set new, more ambitious goals over time.

Building a Legacy of Integrity and Impact

Sustainability and social responsibility aren't just trends; they are the foundation of lasting success and integrity in business. Through these principles, we create businesses that not only serve our own goals but also uplift our communities, care for our planet, and inspire others

Reflecting on my own journey, I've seen that every effort, however small, can lead to meaningful change. From reusing resources to giving back to the community, every decision has the potential to create a positive ripple effect. As you move forward in your business, remember that success isn't measured only by profit but by the impact you leave behind. By building a business rooted in sustainable and responsible practices, you're not only setting yourself up for success but contributing to a better world for generations to come.

Reflection Questions and Exercises

Reflecting on your current sustainability practices is a vital step in ensuring your business is on the right path toward making a positive impact. Here are some thought-provoking questions and practical exercises to guide your self-assessment and foster improvement.

Reflection Questions

➜ **What sustainability practices do you currently have in place?**
Consider how they align with your business goals and values. Are they effective?

➜ **Who are your key stakeholders, and how do they perceive your sustainability efforts?**
Engage them in conversations to gather insights and feedback.

➜ **What are the most significant environmental impacts of your operations?**
Identify areas where you can reduce waste, energy consumption, or carbon emissions.

➜ **How do your employees perceive sustainability in your workplace?**
Conduct surveys or informal discussions to understand their views and suggestions.

➜ **What are your competitors doing in terms of**

sustainability?
Analyze their practices and consider how you can differentiate yourself while enhancing your efforts.

Practical Exercises

➜ **Conduct a Sustainability Audit:**
Evaluate your current operations against sustainability benchmarks. Identify strengths and areas for improvement.

➜ **Create a Sustainability Action Plan:**
Outline specific, measurable goals for your sustainability initiatives, along with timelines and responsibilities.

➜ **Engage Your Team:**
Organize a brainstorming session to gather ideas from your employees on how to improve sustainability in the workplace.

➜ **Develop Partnerships:**
Reach out to local organizations or businesses that align with your sustainability goals and explore collaboration opportunities.

➜ **Track Your Progress:**
Set up a system to monitor the effectiveness of your sustainability initiatives regularly, making adjustments as needed.

Checklist for Immediate Application

To enhance sustainability in your business, consider implementing the following actionable steps:

→ **Evaluate Your Current Practices:**
  - ☐ Review existing sustainability initiatives and identify gaps that need addressing.

→ **Set Clear Sustainability Goals:**
  - ☐ Define specific, measurable targets for reducing waste, energy use, and carbon emissions.

→ **Engage Employees:**
  - ☐ Foster a culture of sustainability by involving your team in discussions and initiatives. Provide training on eco-friendly practices.

→ **Adopt Eco-Friendly Materials:**
  - ☐ Transition to sustainable materials and suppliers that prioritize ethical practices.

→ **Implement Energy Efficiency Measures:**
  - ☐ Upgrade to energy-efficient lighting, appliances, and systems to reduce energy consumption.

→ **Launch a Recycling Program:**
  - ☐ Set up a comprehensive recycling system

for paper, plastics, and other materials in your workplace.

➜ Communicate Your Efforts:

- ☐ Share your sustainability initiatives with stakeholders through newsletters, social media, or your website to build awareness and trust.

➜ Monitor and Measure Impact:

- ☐ Establish metrics to track the effectiveness of your sustainability efforts and regularly report on progress.

➜ Stay Informed:

- ☐ Keep up-to-date with industry trends and innovations in sustainability to continually improve your practices.

➜ Seek Feedback:

- ☐ Regularly solicit input from employees, customers, and stakeholders on your sustainability efforts, and be open to making changes based on their suggestions.

EMBRACING TECHNOLOGY AND INNOVATION

In the early days of my farming journey, technology was a distant concept; I was focused on day-to-day survival, learning the nuances of agriculture, and making sure each crop or bird thrived. However, over time, I came to see technology as not only useful but essential in achieving efficiency, scaling operations, and even unlocking creative solutions to traditional challenges. Technology transformed my approach, teaching me to work smarter, not just harder.

In this chapter, I'll share my journey of incorporating technology into farming and business, along with practical strategies for embracing technological advancements. Whether you're in agriculture or another field, the principles of adopting relevant technology, integrating it smoothly, and using innovation to drive growth remain the same. Let's explore the transformative power of technology and how it can become your ally in building a forward-thinking, resilient business.

Laying the Groundwork

Technology has become an indispensable part of business today. While it's tempting to think that technology is just for big corporations with massive budgets, the truth is that small businesses can (and should) leverage tech just as effectively. For my farm, the introduction of simple technology solutions, from automated systems to digital tools for tracking health, helped me save time and reduce costs, allowing me to focus on the bigger picture. Some of the value and impact on technology in business are

→ **Efficiency and Automation:**
By automating repetitive tasks, technology frees up time and resources for higher-level strategic work. From technical work to process flow. For example, one of our partners uses an automated irrigation system on the farm. This reduced water usage and minimized the time spent manually watering crops. That was innovation. There are also softwares to aid in automating process flow. Like zapier and make.com They automate tasks like email marketing and customer support.

→ **Data-Driven Decision-Making:**
Technology allows us to collect, analyze, and interpret data that can guide smarter decisions. On the farm, tracking data on crop yields, and egg production rate helped me make informed choices about seasonal planting and feed adjustments.

→ **Improved Communication and Collaboration:**
Technology bridges the gap between teams, suppliers, and customers, streamlining interactions and making communication easier and faster. With messaging apps, I stayed in touch with suppliers and could troubleshoot issues quickly, minimizing downtime.

Choosing Tools That Truly Add Value

The challenge with technology is that it can sometimes feel overwhelming, with new tools and platforms emerging every day. However, not every technology is necessary or even useful for every business. The key lies in selecting technologies that genuinely add value to your business model. In farming, this might look like choosing GPS-based soil mapping over trendy but non-essential gadgets. In other industries, it could mean opting for simple, effective software that enhances productivity over flashy, complex systems that don't address real needs. Here's a quick guide to identifying the right technology for your business:

→ **Assess Your Current Challenges and Needs:** Start by identifying the specific areas of your business that need improvement. For me, the goal was to streamline sales and feed monitoring systems. By identifying these needs, I could research technologies that addressed them directly.

→ **Research and Seek Expert Advice:** Once you know your needs, investigate available solutions. Talk to other business owners, consult industry experts, and compare options to make informed decisions.

→ **Consider Scalability:** Choose technology that can grow with your business. When I initially invested in logistics tracking software, I opted for a version that allowed me to add more features as the logistics part of the business expanded, saving both time and money in the long run.

Making the Transition Seamless

One of the biggest obstacles to technology adoption is the initial learning curve. Change is never easy, and even beneficial technology can feel daunting to implement. But I learned firsthand that with a little planning and patience, the integration process can be smooth. When I introduced digital inventory management for the farm, there was some initial resistance from my team. However, by training them on the software and   gradually incorporating it into our routine, the technology eventually became second nature. Here's how to ensure a smooth transition:

➜ **Plan and Communicate the Transition:** When introducing new technology, involve your team in the planning process, communicate the benefits clearly, and explain how it will improve their work.

➜ **Provide Training and Support:** Equip your team with the skills they need to use the technology effectively. In my case, training sessions helped everyone understand and feel comfortable with the new systems.

➜ **Start Small and Expand Gradually:** Introduce technology in stages, allowing time for adjustment and troubleshooting. For example, I started with automated tasks on a smaller scale before implementing it across the other processes.

Innovation

Innovation isn't just about adopting the latest tech; it's a mindset that encourages experimentation, creativity, and continuous improvement. It's about finding unique ways to solve problems and improve processes. I embraced innovation when I began testing organic, natural pest control methods rather than relying on chemical sprays. Though it was a small change, it showed me that innovation comes in many forms and doesn't always require advanced technology. Some ways to make innovation part of your strategy include:

➜ **Encourage Creative Thinking:**
Foster an environment where your team feels empowered to suggest ideas and improvements. On my farm we encourage even the simplest ideas, and some of them have led to great improvements.

➜ **Iterate and Improve Constantly**: Make it a habit to review and refine processes. Every season, we reassess our methods, trying to improve efficiency, reduce waste, and increase productivity.

➜ **Take Calculated Risks:** Innovation requires stepping out of your comfort zone. By experimenting with new methods or products, we've often discovered more efficient ways of doing things.

Staying Ahead of the Curve

Technology is rapidly advancing, staying ahead of the curve isn't just about keeping up with trends; it's about anticipating changes and adapting proactively. As I grew in my understanding of technology's role on the farm, I realized that continuous learning and openness to change were essential to staying competitive. To future-proof your business, consider these steps:

→ **Keep Learning:**
   Attend workshops, read industry publications, and stay curious about emerging trends. Learning about advancements in agriculture, for instance, helped me make strategic choices that kept my farm productive and efficient.

→ **Network with Industry Peers:**
   Join groups, forums, or associations where you can discuss trends and best practices with other professionals. Many of the best tips and technology insights I received came from fellow farmers at conferences and meetings.

→ **Invest in Versatile Technology:**
   Opt for technology that can adapt to new needs. For instance, using cloud-based software made it easier to update our tracking system as new features became available, avoiding the hassle

of changing platforms entirely.

Embracing a Mindset of Growth and Adaptability

Embracing technology and innovation isn't just about incorporating new tools or strategies; it's about building a mindset of continuous improvement, flexibility, and foresight. Reflecting on my journey, I've seen how technology and innovation can make a tangible difference, whether by simplifying daily tasks, helping us make better decisions, or opening up new opportunities. Incorporating technology with purpose and intention helps us streamline processes, reduce costs, and stay competitive. Innovation, meanwhile, keeps our businesses agile and prepared to tackle future challenges. Both are necessary ingredients in building a resilient, future-ready business.

Remember, as you implement these principles, stay rooted in the core values that make your business unique. Technology is an incredible tool, but it should always serve the larger vision. By blending adaptability, and innovation, you're setting yourself up for a future where your business isn't just surviving but thriving, ready to face whatever challenges come its way.

Reflection Questions

Questions for Assessing Current Technology Use

➜ What technologies are currently in use within your business? Reflect on the tools and systems that support your daily operations. Are they meeting your needs?

➜ How well do your current technologies integrate with one another? Consider if your tools work seamlessly together or if there are gaps that hinder efficiency.

➜ What feedback have you received from your team about the technology they use? Gather insights from your staff. Their experiences can highlight areas for improvement.

➜ How often do you evaluate and update your technological tools? Ask yourself if you have a regular schedule for assessing your tech stack or if it's been a while since you made any updates.

➜ What specific challenges do you face due to outdated technology? Identify pain points where technology may be holding your business back.

Practical Exercises for Exploring Innovative Solutions

➜ **Conduct a Technology Audit**
Take a week to track how often and for what purpose each technology is used. Evaluate their effectiveness and areas for improvement.

➜ **Brainstorm New Tools**
Set aside time for a team brainstorming session to identify potential new tools or technologies that could enhance operations. Encourage creativity and open-mindedness.

➜ **Create a Technology Wish List**
Have each team member list three technologies they believe could improve their work experience. Review and discuss as a team to prioritize potential solutions.

➜ **Pilot a New Tool**
Choose one new technology that seems promising and run a pilot program for a month. Gather feedback and assess its impact on productivity and team satisfaction.

➜ **Engage in Online Courses**
Encourage your team to enroll in online courses focused on emerging technologies relevant to your industry. This investment in knowledge can spark innovative ideas.

Checklist for Immediate Application

Steps to Enhance Technology Integration in Your Business

→ **Evaluate Current Technology**
   ☐ Conduct a thorough assessment of the technologies you're currently using.
   ☐ Are they still effective?

→ **Set Clear Goals**
   ☐ Define specific goals for what you want to achieve with new technology. This could be improving efficiency, enhancing customer experience, or streamlining communication.

→ **Research New Solutions**
   ☐ Spend time researching tools and technologies that align with your goals.
   ☐ Read reviews, watch demos, and reach out to vendors.

→ **Involve Your Team**
   ☐ Gather input from your team regarding technology needs and preferences. Involvement leads to better buy-in and effective integration.

→ **Develop an Implementation Plan**
   ☐ Outline a clear plan for integrating new technologies, including timelines, responsibilities, and training sessions.

➜ **Provide Training**

- ☐ Ensure your team has the necessary training to use new tools effectively.
- ☐ Offer ongoing support as they transition.

➜ **Monitor Progress**

- ☐ After implementation, regularly monitor the technology's effectiveness.
- ☐ Collect feedback from your team and make adjustments as needed.

➜ **Encourage Innovation**

- ☐ Foster a culture of innovation by encouraging team members to share new ideas and suggestions for using technology in creative ways.

➜ **Stay Informed**

- ☐ Keep abreast of technological advancements in your industry. Subscribe to relevant newsletters, join forums, and attend webinars.

➜ **Reflect and Adapt**

- ☐ Schedule regular reflection sessions to assess technology's impact on your business and make changes as necessary.

MEASURING SUCCESS & CONTINUOUS IMPROVEMENT

In business, understanding what success looks like isn't always straightforward. Early on in my journey, my farm's "success" was simply measured by whether I could sustain it season after season. With time, however, I learned that real success was about more than survival, it involved setting tangible goals, measuring progress, and consistently improving. This chapter explores how to effectively measure success through clear metrics and key performance indicators (KPIs) and strategies to make continuous improvement a core part of your business model. Whether you're in agriculture, retail, or any other field, measuring your progress is essential to scaling your vision and staying competitive. Here, I'll share insights from my farming and entrepreneurial journey, offering a balanced approach to measuring growth and ensuring it aligns with your mission and values. The first step in measuring success is understanding what success means to you. For a long time, my personal goal in farming was simple: produce a quality yield while managing costs. However, as my business grew, my understanding of success evolved to include profitability, customer satisfaction, and sustainability. Success metrics can be both quantitative (like revenue) and qualitative (like customer loyalty). Here's a breakdown of defining these for your business:

→ **Align with Your Vision:**
  Start by revisiting your vision and mission. For me, success meant not only running a profitable farm but creating a community-centered enterprise. This vision influenced my metrics.

→ **Set Short-Term and Long-Term Goals:**
Success in business isn't a single destination; it's a journey. I learned to set short-term goals, like reducing feed costs by 10% each season, and long-term goals, such as expanding to a larger market.

→ **Focus on What Matters Most:** It's easy to get caught up in vanity metrics that don't impact the bottom line. Instead, choose metrics that directly relate to your growth, like customer retention rate or profit margins.

Tracking the Right Metrics

Key Performance Indicators (KPIs) are quantifiable measures that reflect the performance of key aspects of your business. For me, early KPIs were straightforward, like the rate of egg production or crop yield per season. Over time, I started tracking more nuanced indicators, such as feed efficiency and customer satisfaction, which offered deeper insights into business health. Here's a guide to creating effective KPIs for your business:

→ **Identify Core KPIs:**
Select KPIs that directly align with your core operations. For a farm, this means tracking yield per acre; for a retail store, it might be sales per customer.

→ **Quantify and Set Benchmarks:**
KPIs work best when you have a standard to

measure them against. In farming, I set benchmarks based on seasonal performance, allowing me to adjust targets as conditions and market demands changed.

➜ **Balance Financial and Operational KPIs:** While revenue and profits are critical, operational KPIs like inventory turnover and customer satisfaction can provide insight into daily efficiency and potential areas for improvement. Some practical KPIs for most businesses include:

- Revenue growth
- Customer retention rate
- Operational costs
- Employee productivity and satisfaction
- Profit margins

Empowering Data-Driven Decisions

Collecting data is only useful if you can interpret it effectively. Initially, I tracked metrics by hand, jotting down expenses, yields, and sales numbers in notebooks. But as my farm and team grew, so did the need for more sophisticated tracking tools. Introducing data management tools, from spreadsheets to more specialized software, made a noticeable difference in my decision-making and allowed me to operate more strategically. Here are some tools and strategies to consider:

➜ **Spreadsheets for Basic Tracking:**
Start with Excel or Google Sheets for a
cost-effective and versatile solution.
Spreadsheets work well for tracking monthly
revenue, expenses, and simple operational data.

➜ **Industry-Specific Software:**
For farming, tools that monitor weather, yield,
and chicken health gave me valuable insights.
Look for software that caters to your industry's
unique needs.

➜ **Customer Relationship Management (CRM)
Tools:**
If customer satisfaction is a core KPI, CRM
software can track interactions, complaints, and
purchase history, allowing you to tailor customer
experiences.

➜ **Financial Analysis Software:**
Tools like QuickBooks help with detailed financial
tracking and analysis, giving you insights into
cash flow and overall financial health.

Embracing a Growth Mindset

One of the most significant lessons I learned from
farming is that every season is different. Weather
patterns, soil quality, and market demand fluctuate
constantly, and to thrive, I had to adapt. The mindset of
continuous improvement is essential for any business.

Committing to learning and refining your practices helps you stay resilient and competitive, regardless of your industry. Some practical improvement strategies include:

➜ **Regular Performance Reviews:**
   At the end of each season, I assess what went well and what didn't. Translate this into business terms by reviewing your KPIs monthly, quarterly, or yearly, depending on your needs.

➜ **Encourage Feedback Loops:**
   Gather input from your team and customers. I often received valuable feedback from clients, which allowed me to adjust services accordingly.

➜ **Experiment and Innovate:**
   Trial and error are invaluable for growth. By testing new practices and embracing the occasional setback, I've found new ways to save costs and improve efficiency. In business, don't be afraid to try new marketing strategies or adjust your product offerings based on market feedback.

Recognizing Milestones and Motivating Growth

Celebrating successes, both big and small, is crucial for maintaining morale and recognizing progress. On the farm, we celebrate milestones like reaching a new yield target or securing a big client. Celebrating fosters a sense of accomplishment and reinforces the importance of each step along the journey. Incorporating celebrations in your business can look like:

→ **Setting Milestone Rewards:**
When I achieved specific milestones, like increasing my poultry stock by 20%, I treated myself and the team to a small celebration. Recognize your own achievements and make it a practice to reward team efforts, whether through team lunches or small bonuses.

→ **Reflect on Growth:**
Take time to acknowledge how far you've come. Reflecting on personal growth and improvements over time adds perspective and helps you stay motivated for the next chapter of your business.

→ **Share Success Stories:**
Share accomplishments with your customers and team. Doing so can reinforce loyalty and strengthen your brand's reputation.

Cultivating Success and Improvement

Success in business is a journey, not a destination. Like nurturing a crop, it takes patience, care, and constant adjustment. Measuring success, setting tangible goals, and committing to continuous improvement can help ensure that your business not only grows but thrives. Remember that success isn't just about hitting financial targets; it's about aligning with your values, improving steadily, and contributing positively to those around you. As you apply these strategies, stay grounded in your unique vision and purpose. Your journey will have its highs and lows, but by measuring success thoughtfully and embracing a mindset of continuous growth, you're building a foundation for lasting success. Let every season, every challenge, and every victory be a reminder of how far you've come and an encouragement for the road ahead.

Reflection Questions and Exercises

→ **What does success look like for you?**
Take a moment to reflect on your vision of success. How does it align with your current business goals? Write down your thoughts and share them with your team to encourage discussion.

→ **What KPIs are you currently using, and do they reflect your priorities?**
Evaluate your existing KPIs. Are they truly measuring what matters most to your business? Consider setting aside time for a team brainstorming session to identify any new KPIs that might be more relevant.

→ **How often do you analyze your data, and what tools do you use?**
Reflect on your current data analysis practices. Are your tools effectively providing you with the insights you need? If not, research new tools that could better serve your needs and consider piloting them.

→ **What feedback mechanisms do you have in place?** Assess the effectiveness of your feedback loops.

Practical Exercises for Developing Continuous Improvement Plans

1. **Conduct a SWOT Analysis with Your Team**
    Set aside time for a team workshop to analyze your business's Strengths, Weaknesses, Opportunities, and Threats (SWOT). Break into small groups and assign each one of these four areas, then bring everyone back together to discuss findings. Use this SWOT analysis as a foundation to identify areas that could benefit from continuous improvement initiatives. This exercise will help reveal where your strengths can be maximized and where weaknesses can be improved upon.

2. **Set Up a "Continuous Improvement" Brainstorming Session**
    Encourage your team to share improvement ideas with no limitations on feasibility at first. Assign a moderator to guide the conversation but keep the brainstorming open-ended. Afterward, categorize these ideas into short-term and long-term possibilities. This exercise encourages team engagement and allows everyone to feel like a contributor to the business's growth.

→ **Create a Process Map for a Key Business Function**
    Choose a critical business function like customer service, product delivery, or billing and work with your team to map out every step in the process.

Document each stage, discuss pain points, and look for steps that can be streamlined. This process map can serve as a reference tool and reveal opportunities for enhancement, creating a foundation for regular evaluation and improvement.

→ **Implement a "PDCA" (Plan-Do-Check-Act) Cycle**
Identify a small, manageable project and apply the PDCA cycle to it. Plan a change, execute it (Do), check the results, and act based on what you've learned. This exercise familiarizes the team with iterative improvement and helps them see the tangible results of continuous improvement efforts in a structured way.

→ **Monthly Reflection and Goal-Setting Sessions**
Schedule a monthly reflection meeting where you and your team review what went well, what could have been improved, and set goals for the coming month. Over time, this becomes a feedback loop that feeds into your continuous improvement plans. This regular practice reinforces the importance of setting, measuring, and refining your goals as part of a proactive improvement culture.

Checklist for Immediate Application

☐ **Define Key Metrics and KPIs for Success**
Identify and document your key performance indicators (KPIs) aligned with your business objectives. Select a mix of financial, customer, and operational metrics to capture a holistic view of performance. Set targets for each KPI and ensure they are measurable and attainable.

☐ **Choose the Right Tools for Measurement and Data Analysis**
Assess the tools you currently use for data collection and analysis. Identify gaps or limitations and, if needed, research new tools that provide more relevant insights. For example, consider implementing Google Analytics for web data, CRM software for customer insights, or accounting software for real-time financial tracking.

☐ **Establish a Regular Review Schedule for Performance Metrics**
Set a regular schedule weekly, monthly, or quarterly to review key metrics with your team. Use these sessions to identify trends, assess progress, and discuss any adjustments needed to stay aligned with your business goals.

☐ **Develop a Feedback Loop with Your Team and Customers**

Enccurage open communication with both your team and customers. Set up a system to gather feedback regularly, whether through surveys, reviews, or one-on-one check-ins. Make sure you review this feedback promptly and look for recurring themes or areas that need attention.

☐ **Implement a Small Improvement Project Using the PDCA Cycle**
Select a small, low-risk project to test out the PDCA cycle. Use it to address a specific issue or make a minor process improvement. Document each step and track results. If the project is successful, expand the approach to larger areas of the business.

☐ **Celebrate Small Wins and Recognize Team Efforts Regularly**
Make it a habit to acknowledge achievements, whether a team member hitting a target, completing a project, or even offering an innovative idea. Recognize these efforts in team meetings, with small rewards, or a note of appreciation. Regular acknowledgment encourages motivation and a sense of ownership.

☐ **Document and Track Continuous Improvement Progress**
Create a log for continuous improvement initiatives where you document projects, track their progress,

MAKING DECISIONS WITH PURPOSE AND CLARITY

As entrepreneurs, decision-making can often feel overwhelming. We face countless choices that can lead to both triumphs and setbacks. Over the years, I've come to realize that my faith has been a compass guiding me through the fog of uncertainty. In this chapter, I'll share how my spiritual beliefs have influenced my decision-making process and how you can harness your faith to find clarity and purpose in your business journey.

Through personal stories and practical insights, I hope to inspire you to lean into your beliefs as you navigate the complexities of entrepreneurship.

Understanding the Role of Faith in Decision-Making

Faith is more than just a belief; it's a foundation upon which we can build our lives and businesses. It provides us with a sense of purpose, clarity, and direction, particularly during challenging times. For me, faith is like a lighthouse guiding me through turbulent waters, helping me maintain focus and find my way back to calmer shores. Let me illustrate this with a personal story. During the early days of my poultry farming venture, I faced a critical decision about whether to expand my operations. I had the opportunity to acquire a larger facility, which promised increased production. However, the financial risk was substantial. I prayed about it, seeking guidance and clarity. Through scripture and quiet reflection, I felt a sense of peace about the decision, combined with a caution that urged me to consider all factors carefully. Ultimately, I made the decision to expand, but not without conducting thorough research, developing a solid plan, and trusting in the guidance I received through prayer. This experience reinforced my belief that faith, combined with thoughtful analysis, can lead to sound decisions.

Seeking Clarity Through Prayer and Reflection

When faced with important decisions, taking the time to pray and reflect can provide the clarity needed to move forward. Prayer has been a cornerstone of my decision-making process, helping me align my choices with my values and beliefs. For example, there was a time when I was considering diversifying my crop production. While I had a strong background in poultry, venturing into crop farming was relatively new territory for me. I felt a mixture of excitement and apprehension. Instead of rushing into this new venture, I dedicated time to pray and reflect on my motivations and goals. I asked myself questions like: "What is my intention for this expansion?" and "How will this align with my overall vision for my business?" Through this process, I gained clarity. I realized that diversifying would not only spread risk but also provide fresh opportunities for growth. With a clear sense of purpose, I began researching which crops would complement my existing operations and how to best implement this new strategy.

Making Decisions Aligned with Core Values

Faith is deeply intertwined with our values, and aligning our decisions with these core beliefs is essential for authentic and purpose-driven entrepreneurship. When your choices resonate with your values, you cultivate integrity and trust within your business. During a particularly trying season, I faced ethical dilemmas regarding sourcing supplies for my poultry operation. I was approached by suppliers offering lower-quality feed at a reduced cost. While the immediate financial benefit was tempting, it conflicted with my commitment to animal welfare and sustainability. I prayed for wisdom and sought advice from fellow farmers who shared my values. Ultimately, I chose to stick with suppliers who upheld my standards, even if it meant higher costs in the short term. This decision not only aligned with my values but also strengthened my brand reputation and customer trust. My faith encouraged me to prioritize integrity, and I was reminded that doing the right thing often yields long-term benefits.

Trusting in Uncertainty

In entrepreneurship, uncertainty is a constant companion. There will be times when you must make decisions without all the information or assurances you desire. In these moments, trusting your faith can provide a solid foundation. During a particularly challenging season, I faced unforeseen circumstances, a sudden market downturn, coupled with unexpected weather events that threatened my crops. Fear and doubt began to creep in, and I found myself second-guessing my choices. In the midst of this turmoil, I turned to my faith for strength. I remembered the biblical promise found in Philippians 4:6-7, which encourages us not to be anxious but to present our requests to God. I took comfort in knowing that I was not alone in my struggles. I prayed for guidance, seeking clarity and peace amidst the storm. Over time, I realized that while I couldn't control external factors, I could control my response. I focused on adapting my business strategy, exploring new markets, and building relationships within my community. This shift in perspective, grounded in faith, allowed me to navigate uncertainty with confidence and resilience.

Creating a Decision-Making Framework Guided by Faith

To effectively integrate faith into your decision-making process, it's helpful to establish a framework. Here are some steps you can take:

→ **Define Your Values:**
   Clearly articulate your core values and beliefs. This will serve as a compass when making decisions. Reflect on how these values align with your vision for your business.

→ **Incorporate Prayer and Reflection:**
   Set aside time for prayer and reflection before making significant decisions. This practice can help you gain insight and peace as you navigate

your choices.

→ **Seek Wisdom from Others:**
Don't hesitate to reach out to mentors, fellow entrepreneurs, or spiritual leaders for guidance. Their perspectives can provide valuable insights and encourage you to consider aspects you may have overlooked.

→ **Evaluate Outcomes:**
After making a decision, evaluate the outcomes. Reflect on what worked, what didn't, and how your faith influenced your choices. This continuous learning process will refine your decision-making skills over time.

Incorporating faith into your decision-making process can lead to greater clarity, purpose, and alignment with your values. As you navigate the complexities of entrepreneurship, remember that faith is not just a passive belief but an active force guiding you toward meaningful choices.

Embrace the journey of making decisions rooted in purpose and clarity, and trust that your faith will lead you on a path of growth and success. As you face challenges and opportunities, let your beliefs illuminate the way forward. With faith as your guide, you can make decisions that not only benefit your business but also align with your deeper purpose, creating a fulfilling and impactful entrepreneurial journey.

PREPARING FOR FUTURE CHALLENGES AND OPPORTUNITIES

While we cannot predict every challenge that may arise, we can prepare ourselves to navigate them effectively. This preparation requires a proactive mindset, one that anticipates potential obstacles and formulates strategies to address them. For instance, as I expanded my poultry farming operations, I encountered various regulatory changes that could have impacted my business. Instead of waiting for the changes to occur, I invested time in understanding the regulations, attending workshops, and engaging with industry experts. This proactive approach allowed me to adjust my practices ahead of time, ensuring compliance and minimizing disruption.

In business, preparation also involves financial planning. Having a robust financial plan in place can serve as a safety net during turbulent times. I learned this the hard way during an economic downturn when my cash flow was severely impacted. I had to scramble to find solutions, but if I had anticipated the possibility and built reserves, the transition would have been smoother.

A growth-oriented perspective is essential for thriving in the face of change. As you look toward the future, embrace a mindset that welcomes challenges as opportunities for growth. This means being open to learning, seeking feedback, and continuously improving your skills and knowledge. I recall a time when I faced criticism from my peers regarding my marketing approach. Initially, I felt defensive and discouraged.

However, after taking some time to reflect, I realized that their feedback could help me grow. I sought advice from mentors and attended marketing workshops to enhance my understanding. This experience not only improved my marketing strategy but also reinforced the importance of a growth mindset.

In your journey, remember that every setback can be a stepping stone. Embrace challenges as opportunities to learn and evolve, and you'll find yourself better prepared for whatever lies ahead.

As entrepreneurs, we are not alone on this journey. Building a strong network of support can provide invaluable resources and encouragement during challenging times. Surround yourself with fellow entrepreneurs, mentors, and supportive friends who can offer guidance, share experiences, and celebrate successes with you.

I've learned the power of community firsthand. When I faced a particularly challenging year in my farming business, it was my network that lifted me up. I participated in local farmer cooperatives and networking events, where I connected with others who faced similar struggles. Sharing our stories and solutions not only inspired me but also opened doors to collaborative opportunities that benefited us all. Investing in relationships and cultivating a supportive network can provide the emotional and practical support needed to navigate the entrepreneurial landscape. As you move forward, seek out opportunities to connect with others and build a community that shares your values and vision.

Conclusion

As you embark on your entrepreneurial journey, remember that the path ahead is filled with potential. Embrace the challenges and opportunities that come your way, and let your faith be your anchor during turbulent times. The lessons you've learned and the experiences you've gained will shape your journey, allowing you to navigate the ever-changing landscape of entrepreneurship with resilience and grace.

Your journey is unique, and your story is unfolding. Approach each day with a sense of curiosity and a willingness to adapt. Trust that you are equipped with the tools, insights, and faith to thrive. Together, let us embrace the journey ahead, cultivating not only successful businesses but also meaningful lives that reflect our values and impact our communities.

Thank you for joining me on this journey. I hope this book has provided you with practical insights and inspiration as you forge your own path in the world of entrepreneurship. Remember, the journey is ongoing, and every step you take brings you closer to fulfilling your purpose. Keep moving forward, stay true to your faith, and embrace the incredible opportunities that lie ahead.

Acknowledgement

First and foremost, I thank God for empowering me with the vision, guidance, and resilience to bring this book to completion. My family, mentors, and friends have been pillars of strength, each one of them inspiring me, in ways big and small, to write and share this journey. To the customers who believed in my work from day one, the community members who offered support and encouragement, and to each reader, thank you for being a part of this story.

Your trust and engagement keep me passionate and motivated to grow, evolve, and sow seeds for a more abundant tomorrow. Writing "Harvesting Success" was as much a journey of discovery as it was a labor of love, bringing together years of firsthand experience and personal lessons learned in the fields. I hope this book serves you effectively